GUIDE TO INDIA

BRIAN WILLIAMS

Highlights for Children

CONTENTS

On the cover: The Taj Mahal in Agra, a masterpiece of Indian Mogul architecture and one of the Wonders of the World

Published by Highlights for Children
© 1996 Highlights for Children, Inc.
P.O. Box 18201
Columbus, Ohio 43218-0201

10 9 8 7 6 5 4 3
ISBN 0-87534-922-6

NORTH AMERICA

Tropic of Cancer

Equator

SOUTH AMERICA

Tropic of Capricorn

EUROPE

ASIA

AFRICA

India

AUSTRALIA

ANTARCTICA

△ **India's flag** The wheel in the center is an ancient symbol. This flag, with its green, white, and orange stripes, has been India's national flag since 1947.

INDIA AT A GLANCE

Area 1,269,346 square miles (3,287,263 square kilometers)

Population 913,070,000

Capital New Delhi, population with Old Delhi is 8,370,500

Other big cities Bombay (12,570,000), Calcutta (10,860,000), Madras (5,360,000), Hyderabad (4,270,000)

Highest mountains Kanchenjunga on the border with Nepal, 28,208 feet (8,598 meters); Nanda Devi, 25,646 feet (7,817 meters)

Longest rivers Brahmaputra, section crossing India 1,800 miles (2,900 kilometers), and Ganges, 1,557 miles (2,506 kilometers)

Largest lake There are no large natural lakes in India.

Official language Hindi

▽ **Indian stamps** Shown here are stamps representing Children's Day, the Indian National Archives, a cheerful frog, and some birds of India.

◁ **Indian money** The currency of India is the rupee. This 50-rupee note shows the state emblem with four lions, standing back to back. On the reverse side is a picture of India's Parliament House in New Delhi.

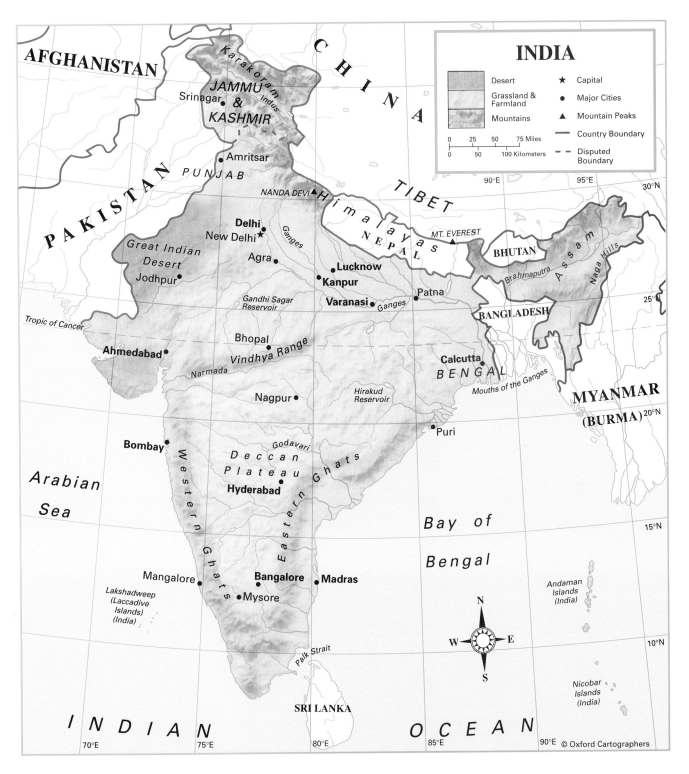

AFGHANISTAN

CHINA

Karakoram

JAMMU
&
KASHMIR

Srinagar

Indus

PAKISTAN

Amritsar

PUNJAB

TIBET

NANDA DEVI ▲ Himalayas

NEPAL

MT. EVEREST ▲

BHUTAN

Delhi

New Delhi ★

Ganges

Lucknow

Agra

Kanpur

Great Indian
Desert

Patna

Jodhpur

Gandhi Sagar
Reservoir

Varanasi

Ganges

BANGLADESH

Brahmaputra

Assam

Naga Hills

Tropic of Cancer

Bhopal

Ahmedabad

Vindhya Range

Narmada

Nagpur

Hirakud
Reservoir

Calcutta

BENGAL

Mouths of the Ganges

MYANMAR
(BURMA) 20°N

Puri

Bombay

Godavari

Deccan
Plateau

Western Ghats

Eastern Ghats

Hyderabad

Arabian

Sea

Bay of

Bengal

Andaman
Islands
(India)

Mangalore

Bangalore

Madras

Lakshadweep
(Laccadive
Islands)
(India)

Mysore

N

W   E

S

Nicobar
Islands
(India)

Palk Strait

SRI LANKA

INDIAN

70°E   75°E   80°E

OCEAN

85°E   90°E © Oxford Cartographers

INDIA

Desert

Grassland &
Farmland

Mountains

★ Capital

● Major Cities

▲ Mountain Peaks

— Country Boundary

- - Disputed
     Boundary

0   25   50   75 Miles
0   50   100 Kilometers

90°E   95°E   30°N

25°N

15°N

10°N

WELCOME TO INDIA

The Republic of India is one of the world's largest countries. It covers most of the central region of southern Asia. India is closed in on the north by the world's tallest mountain range, the Himalayas. On its other sides it is surrounded by the Indian Ocean.

India's landscapes include mountains, deserts, thick jungles, and wide plains. Great rivers flow southward from the Himalayas. There is good farmland in the river valleys. Most of India has a hot climate. There is a long dry season. Then the rains are blown in from the oceans by the monsoon winds.

One out of every six people in the world lives in India. Of the world's nations, only China has more people. India's people belong to different races, speak different languages, and have different religions.

Many Indians live in villages. In the countryside nearly everyone farms and grows their own food. Millions crowd the big cities, such as Dehli, Calcutta, and Bombay. These cities are centers for business and industry. But even on busy city streets, the cars and trucks jostle for space with walkers, bicyclists, and wandering cows.

◁ **Women harvesting wheat** India's main foods are rice, wheat, millet, beans, fruits, and vegetables. Some people also eat meat, fish, and eggs.

▷ **The Charminar building in the city of Hyderabad** Built for a Muslim ruler in the late 1500s, this city is famous for its beautiful gardens, palaces, and avenues.

▷ **A herd of goats near Manali** In the Himalayan countryside, goats are raised for their milk, wool, meat, and hides (leather).

India is thousands of years old. Major religions — Hinduism, Buddhism, Jainism, and Sikhism — began in India. Empires have risen and fallen here. Travelers from all over the world still marvel at the wonders of India. These include ancient artworks and temples, wonderful scenery, and rich wildlife. Tigers, elephants, and one-horned rhinoceros live here, as well as many types of birds, snakes, other reptiles, and insects. Tourists visiting India today can enjoy all these sights and sounds. Here is a land with much to see. Come and explore India.

DELHI, CITY OF GOVERNMENT

The city of Delhi is the capital of India. Delhi lies on the west bank of the Yamuna River. There are actually two cities of Delhi. Old Delhi is more than 500 years old. It has a busy industrial section, but also many old narrow streets. More than eight million people live in Delhi.

New Delhi is very different. British planners designed the city in the early 1900s. One of the buildings designed by the British is now the home of the President of India. A large circular building contains the two houses of the Indian Parliament.

If you ask directions in Delhi, people will be friendly and may answer in English. Hindi is India's official language, but many people understand and speak English.

People come to Delhi to visit the museums and walk the Rajpath. Along this avenue, the big event is the Republic Day Parade on January 26. It includes cultural pagents from each of India's states. Delhi also has a fine zoo, famous for its rare white tigers. South of New Dehli people climb the Qutab Minar, a tall red tower built in the 1200s. There are 376 steps to the top.

After sightseeing, rest in the nearby park and admire the brilliantly colored peacocks. The peacock is India's national bird. In the park, you may also see boys hitting small balls with wooden bats on dusty playgrounds. They are playing cricket, India's most popular sport.

Indian food has many flavors. In the restaurants of Delhi, diners enjoy spicy curries, vegetables, lentils, tasty kebabs, and dishes of chicken and mutton cooked slowly in a clay oven called a *tandoor*.

▷ **A view across New Delhi** India's capital city is an important industrial center as well as the heart of government.

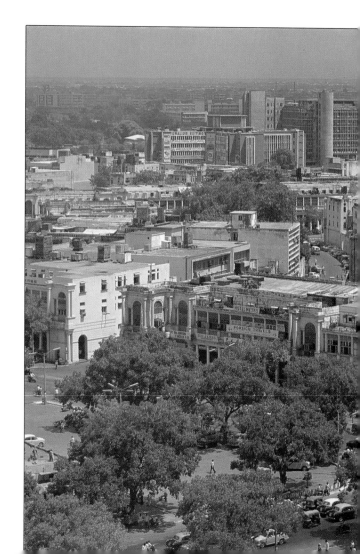

◁ **Mohandas K. Gandhi**
This statue honors Gandhi and the people he led on a protest march against British rule in 1930.

▽ **The Jama Masjid mosque in Delhi** Like the nearby Red Fort, it was built for the emperor Shah Jahan. It is the biggest mosque in India, big enough for 25,000 Muslim worshipers.

MOUNTAINS AND TEMPLES

The Yamuna River that flows past Delhi begins in the Himalayan mountains. These are the highest mountains in the world. India shares them with its neighbors China, Bhutan, Pakistan, and Nepal. The Himalayas spread through five Indian states and many others also have hilly areas.

Below the peaks, the mountain slopes are cool and green with trees. In spring, the valleys are bright with colorful flowers and shrubs. Many Himalayan plants were brought to America and Europe in the 1800s and planted in gardens. Mountain rivers, gorges, forests, and valleys offer scenic views. The Vale of Kashmir is a valley so beautiful that the Mogul emperors called it Paradise. The air is sweet with the smell of roses. Hindu pilgrims walk for four days from the tourist center of Pahalgam to Amarnath Cave, a shrine to the god Shiva. There are many other holy shrines and temples in the valley, where people go in large numbers.

Darjeeling, Musoorie, and Nainital are beautiful hill cities. When Britain ruled India, its officials set up a summer capital in the hill city of Simla and were glad to get away from the heat and dust of the plains around Delhi. A railroad built then still winds its way through the foothills.

The state capital of Jammu and Kashmir is Srinagar, a city in the Himalayan mountains. Winter can be cold here. People wear thick clothes, and underneath they carry clay pots filled with hot coals to keep themselves warm. Around Srinagar farmers grow rice in terraced fields on the hillsides. There are also orchards full of apples, cherries, walnuts, and almonds. The fine wool, cashmere, comes from goats that live in the high mountains.

▷ **A view of Simla** Homes are built into the hillside in a long strip overlooking some of the loveliest and most colorful scenery in the world.

◁ **A long mountain walk to market** This girl lives near the Kolahoi glacier in Kashmir.

▽ **A statue of Buddha in a monastery** Buddhism is one of the many religions of India.

LAND OF FIVE RIVERS

In the northwest section of India there is a large flat region known as the Punjab. The name Punjab comes from two Persian words that mean "five rivers." The rivers are the Jhelum, Chenab, Ravi, Beas, and Sutlej. They all flow into the mighty Indus River. For thousands of years people have lived near these rivers.

The Punjab is a major growing area for wheat and rice. But the farther south you travel, the hotter and drier the land usually becomes. Farmers still irrigate their fields by pumping water from underground wells.

△ **Women draw water from a well** Few people live in the Thar, or Great Indian Desert. But new irrigation projects are attracting farmers to settle there.

◁ **Jodhpur** This city is a busy road and rail junction. Jodhpur gave its name to the tight breeches worn by some horseriders.

▷ **The City Palace at Udaipur** The kings of Rajasthan built two grand palaces on islands in Lake Pichola. Here they kept cool in the summer heat.

The state of Punjab is home to many of India's Sikh people. The Sikhs are followers of a religion founded about 500 years ago. The Golden Temple at Amritsar is their holiest shrine. Sikh men wear turbans. The symbols of the Sikh religion are known as the "five Ks." These are: uncut hair (*kesh*), short pants (*kachha*), an iron bangle (*kara*), a dagger (*kirpan*), and a comb (*kangha*).

Southwest of the Punjab is the state of Rajasthan. Much of the land here is too dry for farming. Mines produce zinc, copper, marble, and granite.

Tourists can ride camels into the scorching Thar desert. In game reserves they may spot tigers, leopards, sambhar deer, wild boars, and Indian bustards.

Rajah means king. In Rajasthan, the land of kings, there are forts, palaces, and temples. Jaipur, the capital of Rajasthan, is called the Pink City after the color of its buildings. One of these, the Palace of the Winds, has 953 windows looking on to the streets. Rajasthan is now a busy industrial region, with chemical plants, electronics factories, and railroad engineering plants.

Bombay – Gateway to India

Traveling south along India's west coast, you enjoy a cool ocean breeze. Each year, between June and September, the winds bring the monsoon rains. The rain is so heavy that it often washes roads away. But people welcome the rain, because it means good crops for farmers.

Bombay is a major business center. This is a city of fine old buildings as well as modern ones. You may see a movie crew at work, for Bombay is the biggest movie-producing city in the world. Indians love the movies. An average of nine million movie tickets are sold every day in India.

Bombay was founded on seven islands, which have been built over and made into one large area. Portuguese sailors who came here in the 1500s called it Bom Bain, meaning "Good Bay." Bombay grew rich in the 1800s. Its factories made cotton goods for sale in Europe. The city became an important part of the British Empire. The harbor was once a base for British warships. Now it is a main base for the Indian Navy. Join the fun on Chowpatty beach where people play, chat, and eat Bombay's popular snack, *bhelpuri*, and ice cream.

People in Bombay enjoy fast food. Roadside stands and restaurants sell savory snacks. Vegetarian dishes are popular since most Indians eat little or no meat. Workers travel long distances by bus or train to their jobs in the city. Later, men known as *dabbawallas* collect hot lunch boxes from the workers' homes and ride into town to deliver them.

Close to Bombay are some amazing rock sculptures. You can go by boat to Elephanta Island, with its Hindu cave temples cut from solid rock. They are 1,300 years old. There are other ancient rock temples to see at Ellora and at Ajanta.

▷ **The state assembly building in Bombay** It stands on Nariman Point.

▷ **The Ajanta Caves** These cave temples date back more than two thousand years, when the caves were used as shelters by Buddhist monks.

△ **The Gateway of India** This famous arch in Bombay marks a visit by Britain's King George V, then Emperor of India, in 1911.

WESTERN COAST

Southern India has a warm climate, ideal for growing fruits and vegetables. People grow tea and coffee on plantations in the hills. You will also see lots of coconut palms and rubber trees. Many people live near the shore in small villages and towns. But traveling inland through the mountains known as the Western Ghats is well worth the effort. Buses and trucks bump and twist over steep, winding roads.

For long journeys, people with enough money for the fare can ride one of India's express trains, such as the Deccan Queen. India's most popular form of transportation is the train. People who cannot get a seat inside a railroad car often ride on the roof.

At Goa, you might think you are in Portugal. Goa was a Portuguese colony for over 400 years. You see churches, people wearing Sunday-best clothes for services, and busy street cafés.

Many people living along the coast earn their living by fishing. They catch shrimp, mackerel, herring, and sardines. If you are offered Bombay duck, remember that it is not a bird, but a small fish. It is dried and often added to a spicy curry. Curries are a favorite Indian dish, but it is best to try a mild curry to begin with!

In towns and villages people work at handcrafts in their homes. They produce carpets, metal bowls, jewelry, and cotton and silk clothes. Often children help. Other people work in modern factories. Bangalore, the garden city of southern India, has large and important aerospace, electronics, and machine tool plants. Such industry is part of the new India.

◁ **A rubber plantation** The rubber trees are planted in rows. Workers make cuts in the trunks. They return later to collect the sticky sap, which is made into rubber.

▷ **Fishermen in Kerala** They use large Chinese-style nets to catch shrimp and fish that live in shallow waters. The fish are sold at local markets.

◁ **Elephants in Periyar Game Sanctuary**
India is trying to preserve its wildlife. This reserve is home to wild elephants, tigers, leopards, and monkeys.

DANCERS, TANKS, AND FORTS

The small state of Kerala on India's southwest coast is famous for the dance drama Kathakali. Musicians play drums and dancers wearing large skirts and heavy makeup leap out into a temple courtyard. Only men dance the lead roles in Kathakali dances, which tell stories from Hindu scriptures.

Many of the people who live in the southernmost part of India have their own languages. They claim to be the descendants of the Dravidians, who came from central Russia over 3,000 years ago. Further south is the cape, or tip, of India, Kanyakumari, in the state of Tamil Nadu.

Farmers collect rainwater from large tanks. The village tank is a good place for people to meet. They also bathe here. But watch out for a snake coming to cool off. It may be a king cobra, the world's largest poisonous animal.

At the city of Mahabalipuram there are famous Hindu temples with shrines to the gods Vishnu and Shiva.

▽ **Rock carvings at Mahabalipuram** This seaport city in southeastern India has some of the finest Hindu rock carvings.

▽ **The bazaar at Madurai**
Here you can buy drinks, magazines, food, and clothes.

△ **A view of the city of Madurai** This city is southern India's important center of learning and religious traditions.

Madras is the fourth largest of India's cities. The people here speak the Tamil language. Women wear colorful clothing — brightly dyed traditional *saris*. Madras was one of the first British bases in India. British traders built a fort here in the 1600s. Old buildings are reminders of the British Empire, known as the "Raj." Madras has big stores. But the places to shop are the bazaars or markets. Here you can bargain for almost anything, from fine silks to radios. In Madras, you can watch *Bharatanatyam*, a classical dance.

Traveling north, you come to the industrial city of Hyderabad. Once the home of a wealthy prince, Hyderabad has a beautiful Islamic mosque, the Mecca Masjid. The blocks of stone used to build it were so enormous that over 1,000 bullocks, or young bulls, were needed to drag them.

If you are interested in castles, do not miss Golconda. This huge stone fort was built to guard the city of Golconda and its rich diamond mines. According to legend, when the Mogul emperor's army tried to capture the castle in 1786, a dog barked. This barking woke those inside as the emperor's soldiers climbed over the walls, and the fort was saved.

INDIAN VILLAGE LIFE

In the center of India is a vast flat plateau, known as the Deccan. On either side there are mountains, the Ghats. The Deccan is a region of mining, forestry, and farming. Here, most people live in small towns and villages and go out to the fields to work every day. Some homes are simple houses made of dried mud and straw. Richer families build their houses of brick.

At night many people use kerosene lamps to light their homes, although more and more villages now have electricity. The most important place in the village is the well. Few villages have running water.

▽ **A tame elephant at work** You can also take a ride on an elephant. The Indian elephant is smaller than the African elephant.

◁ **Harvesting sugarcane** These workers have collected a large pile of cut cane, ready for processing. Sugarcane is an important crop of India.

▽ **Rice field** Here farmers are using oxen to pull plows to prepare the fields for growing rice, one of India's main crops. Many farmers also use tractors to work the land.

Most people in the villages work on farms. In their houses, they choose to have little furniture and few pots for cooking. Many villages have a shared television set. People regularly gather to watch programs broadcast by satellite.

School is held in the open air or in one classroom. Children are taught that learning and education are the ways to a better life for all. The village has its own council of adults, which makes the rules for everyone.

In India people greet visitors politely, saying *namastey*, with a slight bow and hands folded together in front of them. Sometimes men shake hands, but women usually do not. People willingly share food with a traveler. It is okay to eat with your fingers, but only with your right hand.

Few villages have a post office. For a trip to town, people take the bus — the only form of public transportation in country districts. Bicycles, and some motor scooters, are commonly used.

THE HINDU CULTURE

Eight of every ten Indians are Hindus. This religion affects the way people live and the jobs they do. In the Hindu religion there are four castes, or groups of people. Priests and lawmakers are at the head (top) of the caste system. Next come warriors, followed by farmers and merchants. Laborers make up the fourth of the original castes.

Hindus believe that souls are born and reborn many times. They also believe that animals have souls. To Hindus, cows are sacred animals. No Hindu will eat beef, and cows roam freely through the streets. Being clean is an important part of Hindu religion. Hindus bathe three times every day, usually before meals.

Hindus have many gods. Three of the most important are Brahma, the creator, Vishnu, the preserver of life, and Shiva, the destroyer and rebuilder. People believe Ganesha, the elephant-headed god, helps them to begin important tasks. Villagers hold festivals to celebrate the birth of a favorite god. The Hindu religion has its own calendar, with twelve moon-months and six seasons. People visit shrines, or holy places, with offerings of food and flowers. They give gifts to holy men.

▷ **Bathing in the Ganges River** Hindus bathe here for religious reasons, believing the river water purifies them. They also make offerings of rice, fruit, flowers, and coconuts.

22

▽ **The Sun Temple at Konarak, in Orissa**
Here people once worshiped the Sun god.
It is believed that he drove a fiery chariot
across the sky.

▽ **Jagannath Temple at Puri** The temple is
open to Hindus only. Others can view it from
the roof of a nearby building. Puri is one of
the holiest cities of India.

Hindu festivals are fun, with noisy
parades and parties. The new year begins in
the autumn with Divali, the Festival of
Lights. This is a time for family visits, feasts
with sweet cakes and candies, and gifts to
welcome Lakshmi, goddess of riches and
luck. Children fill little clay lamps with oil.
As dusk falls, they set out their lamps on the
roof, on walls, and along the roadside. The
lights honor the return of an ancient ruler
from exile. Holi is the major spring Hindu
festival. People make bonfires and throw
colored water at one another for fun.

CALCUTTA – CROWDED AND AMAZING

Calcutta is the biggest city in eastern India. Four million people live in the center. Another six million live outside the city. Calcutta is the capital of the state of West Bengal. Its people speak a language called Bengali. They are expert weavers and make beautiful garments from silk and cotton. This was the first region of India to become industrialized in the 1800s. Calcutta was then the capital of British India.

Calcutta is India's main port for trade with the Far East. People of many nations have made their homes in the city. Most of Calcutta is on the east bank of the Hooghly River. The land is flat and swampy. The city is overcrowded, and air and water pollution are serious problems.

Many famous poets, storytellers, film makers, and musicians live in Calcutta. The great poet Rabindranath Tagore lived here.

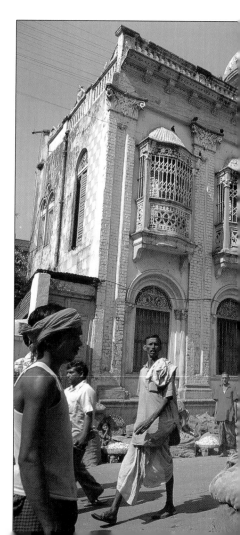

△ **The distant peaks of the Himalayas** From this hilltop near Darjeeling, in West Bengal, you can see several of the world's highest peaks.

▷ **An old house in Calcutta** In front of the home, street traders sell fruit, vegetables, tea, and spices produced by local farmers.

Calcutta was only a village until about 1700. Then Europeans built a trading post here. In the 1700s, the British and Indian rulers fought constantly for control of the region of Bengal. A local ruler, Siraj-ud Daula, captured Calcutta (then known as Fort William) and took more than a hundred Europeans as hostages. But the British won the war in the end, and Calcutta grew around the old fort.

Many people in Calcutta are poor. Yet the city has thriving businesses. The most important are the trade in tea and the processing of jute, a plant fiber used to make sacks. There are also factories making clothes, shoes, and electrical goods.

The city's biggest park is the Maidan. In it stands the Victoria Memorial, named after Victoria, the British queen in the late 1800s. This is a favorite place for picnics.

△ **The Darjeeling railroad** India still has some old steam locomotives. This train is known as the "toy train." When the inside seating is full, passengers hang on to the outside of cars.

INDIA PAST AND PRESENT

Travelers between Calcutta and New Delhi can enjoy air-conditioned comfort on an express train. Long-distance trains stop long enough at stations for people to get out to buy food and drinks. Many also have full-service dining cars.

As you travel through the states of West Bengal and Bihar, you will see many mines. This region produces nearly half of India's minerals, including aluminum, iron ore, and coal. It is also rich in tradition and religious centers. Many travelers head for Varanasi (or Benares) in Uttar Pradesh. Hindus believe this is a holy place. Hindu pilgrims bathe in the Ganges River from a series of steps called *ghats*. When a person dies, the body is burned on a mound called a funeral pyre. The ashes are scattered into the sacred river.

Uttar Pradesh (or U.P. as Indians call it) has more people than any other Indian state. People have lived here since Stone Age times. Scientists hunting for old objects have found prehistoric stone tools.

Kings and emperors of India made this region a stronghold. At Agra is India's most famous building, the Taj Mahal. The emperor Shah Jahan built the Taj Mahal as a tomb for his wife between 1631 and 1648. He, too, is buried beneath its huge dome. Many people think that the Taj Mahal is the most beautiful building in the world. It is certainly one of the most famous.

Twenty miles away from Agra is Fatehpur Sikri. This walled city was the capital of the emperor Akbar the Great, who ruled India in the 1500s. He mixed Indian traditions with new ideas from abroad. In much the same way, modern India joins its rich past to its bright future.

▷ **Morning at the Ganges River** Hindu pilgrims bathe in the river before saying their daily prayers. Here, thousands of pilgrims stand on *ghats* beside the water.

▷ **A Muslim mosque in Lucknow** This city is the capital of Uttar Pradesh to the southeast of Delhi. The building on the right is the tomb of an 18th-century ruler.

△ **A street in Lucknow** Modern traffic and industries are changing India's cities, but the country has saved many fine old buildings.

INDIA FACTS AND FIGURES

People

India's people come from a variety of backgrounds. The two largest groups are Indo-Aryans and the darker-skinned Dravidians. Other groups include Mongoloids in the Himalayan mountains and Nagas and Gonds, peoples who live in hills and forests.

Trade and Industry

Traditional industries include carpets, silk, and other textile products made by people working in their homes. Factories have grown rapidly since the 1950s. Indian factories make cars, bicycles, railroad cars, and sewing machines. There are plants making chemicals, dyes, fertilizers, cement, paper, and food products. India also has iron and steel mills, cotton and jute mills, and oil refineries.

India has valuable minerals, including diamonds and emeralds, iron and aluminum ores, copper, zinc, mica, and sulfur. There is a lot of coal. About 60 percent of India's electricity comes from coal and oil. The rest comes from hydroelectric and nuclear plants.

△ **An Indian banquet** This large variety of food features different regional specialities, including vegetables, fruits, and meat dishes.

Farming

India's chief crops are rice, wheat, coffee, tea, sugarcane, spices, cotton, jute, coconut, and linseed. Two out of every three Indians are farmers. Almost all farms in India are small, and many people do not own the land they farm. Some farmers plow with animals and others with tractors.

Indians grow many fruits, including mangoes, apples, and bananas. India is the world's leading grower of betel nuts (palm nuts that are chewed). Spices grown in India include ginger, pepper, and turmeric.

India has more cattle and water buffalo than any other country. Hindus do not eat beef, but they drink cows' milk.

Floods and droughts sometimes cause farmers problems. But modern methods have brought better harvests. India grows enough food for all its people.

Fishing

Indian fishing boats catch herring, shark, shrimp, and sardines off the coast. Carp and catfish are caught in rivers and ponds.

Food

Most Indians eat little or no meat. The main foods are rice, wheat, millet, peas, and beans. Vegetables are cooked with great care, with blends of spices for flavor. Fresh fruit and fruit drinks are popular. People drink tea or coffee. Sweets are eaten with meals.

Traditional and popular Indian dishes include:

chutney: relish made from fruits and vegetables

curry: vegetables, eggs, meat, or fish, cooked with spices and usually eaten with rice or wheat flat bread called *chappatis*

dal: a porridge made from beans or peas

papadum: thin circle of dough fried crisp in hot oil

samosa: deep-fried pastry filled with either vegetables or meat

Schools

Education in state schools is free for all children between the ages of six and fourteen. About eight out of ten children in India go to school for at least five years.

About a third of all pupils go on to secondary school, but only a small percentage finish their education at a college or university. However, there are more than 5,000 colleges and universities in India.

Country children often do not finish school because they leave to work on family farms. Many adults learn to read on the government's adult education programs.

△ **A statue of the Hindu goddess Durga**
The goddess is shown riding a lion and has eight arms — a sign of power.

The Media

English-language papers include the *Times of India*, *The Hindu*, and *The Statesman*. *Ananda Bazar Patrika* is a Bengali paper published in Calcutta. The *Navbharat Times* is published in the Hindi language. Radio and television services are run by the government. Foreign television is available by satellite.

Art and Drama

India has one of the richest art traditions in the world. Indian sculptors and craftworkers made wonderful stone carvings and monuments thousands of years ago. Painters made pictures for the Mogul emperors, including story-paintings, portraits, battles, and hunting scenes. Jewelers fashioned delicate objects in gold, silver, and precious stones.

Indian dance and music have close links with religion and with drama. Classical dancers use complicated hand and body movements to convey ideas and emotions. Dancers wear bell anklets. There are several dance styles from different parts of India — *Kathak* in the north, *Kathakali* dance dramas of Kerala, the *Bharatanatyam* from the southern states.

There are also regional styles in music. Indian music sounds strange to Western ears. Traditional musical instruments include the *sitar*, a stringed instrument plucked with the fingers, the *sarangi*, played with a bow, and the *tabla*, a pair of drums beaten with the fingers.

INDIA FACTS AND FIGURES

Literature

Indian literature began with religious stories, told out loud. Among the oldest works of Indian literature are the ancient Hindu scriptures, or holy books, the *Vedas*. There are great epic poems written in the ancient Sanskrit language. They include the world's longest poem, the *Mahabharata*, and the *Ramayana*. Later, all Indian languages developed their own literature. From the 1500s Europeans brought printed books and Western styles in poetry and novel writing to India. Famous Indian writers include Rabindranath Tagore, Prem Chand, and R. K. Narayan.

Religion

Religion is important in most Indians' daily lives. Religious rules govern what people eat and how they dress.

More than three-quarters of Indians are Hindus. Hinduism is an unusual religion because it has no single founder or head.

About 11 percent of Indian people are Muslims. There are also Christians, Sikhs, Buddhists, and Jains.

△ **Street traders** Small traders commonly set up shop along roadsides. Here vegetables and spices are on sale.

Festivals

Hindus, Muslims, and people of other religions have their own festivals. These are based on the lunar calendar and fall on different dates each year.

Holi, Dashra, Divali, 'Id-al-Fitr, and Christmas are major festivals. Listed in the next column are India's main national holidays.

January 26 **Republic Day** Commemorates India's constitution, adopted in 1950
August 15 **Independence Day** Marks independence from British rule in 1947
October 2 **Gandhi's Birthday** Honors the great Indian leader Mohandas K. Gandhi

Plants

India has many kinds of forests. In the tropical south, palm trees grow. In the northern mountains, evergreen oaks, chestnut, and rhododendrons are common. There are many beautiful flowers.

Animals

India's large wild animals include elephants, Indian rhinoceros, tigers, and Asiatic lions. There are monkeys, boars, wild oxen, deer, crocodiles, pythons, desert foxes, bats, eagles, bustards, and poisonous cobras and kraits.

Sports

Cricket is India's most popular sport. Indians also enjoy field hockey, wrestling, horse racing, and track and field events.

HISTORY

The first great civilization of India grew up in the Indus Valley, around 2500 B.C. Aryan peoples invaded from the north around 1500 B.C. In the 3rd century B.C. Asoka ruled most of the Indian subcontinent and established Buddhism. But the older Hinduism became the most widely followed religion. Arts and literature enjoyed a golden age during the Gupta kingdom in the 4th to 6th centuries A.D.

Later, Muslim invaders came from the west and north. Muslim Mogul emperors ruled India from 1526 until the 1780s. Great Mogul emperors included Babar, Akbar, and Aurangzeb.

Vasco da Gama sailed to India from Portugal in 1497-98. Europeans began trading in India. They set up bases. Britain became the strongest European power in India. The British government took control of India in 1784 and put down an Indian revolution in 1857. India was called the "jewel in the crown" of the British Empire.

In the early 1900s Mohandas K. Gandhi led a campaign against British rule. Gradually, Gandhi gained more and more rights for Indian people. India eventually became independent in 1947 and two new countries, India and Pakistan, came into being.

Since gaining independence, India has played a leading role in Asian and world affairs. Notable leaders were Jawaharlal Nehru, India's first prime minister, and his daughter Indira Gandhi, who also became prime minister. She was assassinated in 1984. Her son Rajiv replaced her, but he too was assassinated, in 1991.

LANGUAGE

Hindi, in Devnagri script (as written for numbers 1 to 10 in the next column), is the official language of India. English is widely spoken and is the language of business throughout India. There are 17 other languages used in different states.

The languages in northern India belong to the Indo-European language family. Those in the south are Dravidian languages and are not related to the northern languages.

Many Muslims speak Urdu, which is written in Arabic script.

Useful words and phrases

English		Hindi	
1	one	१	ek
2	two	२	dō
3	three	३	teen
4	four	४	char
5	five	५	panch
6	six	६	chē
7	seven	७	saāt
8	eight	८	aath
9	nine	९	nau
10	ten	१०	dās

Useful words and phrases

English	Hindi
Sunday	Raviwar
Monday	Somwar
Tuesday	Mangalwar
Wednesday	Buddhwar
Thursday	Guruwar
Friday	Shukrawar
Saturday	Shaniwar
Greetings/ good-bye	Namastey
Please	Kirpaya
Thank you	Dhanyawad
Yes	Han
No	Nahin
Excuse me	Maaf kijiye

INDEX

Note: Many Indian words, especially names of places and foods, have more than one correct spelling.

Acknowledgments
Book created for Highlights for Children, Inc. by Bender Richardson White.
Editors: Peter MacDonald and Lionel Bender
Designer: Malcolm Smythe
Art Editor: Ben White
Editorial Assistant: Madeleine Samuel
Picture Researcher: Madeleine Samuel
Production: Kim Richardson

Maps produced by Oxford Cartographers, England.
Banknotes from Thomas Cook Currency Services.
Stamps from Stanley Gibbons.

Editorial Consultant: Andrew Gutelle
Guide to India is approved by the Government of India Tourist Office, London
India Consultant: Manorama Jafa, Secretary General, India IBBY, New Delhi
Managing Editor, Highlights New Products: Margie Hayes Richmond

Picture credits
AP/ITB = Audience Planners/Indian Tourist Board. AP/JP = Audience Planners/Joan Pollock. EU = Eye Ubiquitous, Z = Zefa. t = top, b = bottom, l = left, r = right.
Cover: Z. Pages: 6: AP/ITB. 7t, 7b: AP/JP. 8: Z/Vishnu Panjabi. 9t: AP/JP. 9b: AP/ITB. 10-11, 11t, 11b: AP/JP. 12tr, 12bl, 13: AP/JP. 14-15: Z/Starfoto. 15t: AP/JP. 15b: EU/V.C. Sievey.16: AP/ITB. 17t, 17b: AP/JP. 18, 19: AP/ITB. 18-19:EU/David Cumming. 20, 21tr: AP/ITB. 21br: AP/JP. 22: Eye Ubiquitous/David Cumming. 22-23, 23: Eye Ubiquitous/Chris Gibb. 24: AP/JP. 24-25: Z/Sunak. 25: Z/Hugh Ballantyne. 26-27: Eye Ubiquitous/David Cumming. 27t, 27b: Z/Sunak. 28, 29, 30: AP/ITB. *Illustration on page 1* by Tom Powers